SLIM FAST DIET RECIPES

Lose Weight and Feel Great with Delicious Slim Fast Diet Recipes!

Dr. Colin C. Longenecker

Copyright © 2023 Dr. Colin C. Longenecker. All Rights Reserved.

No part of this publication may be reproduced, distributed, or transmitted in any form or by any means, including photocopying, recording, or other electronic or mechanical methods, without the prior written permission of the publisher, except in the case of brief quotations embodied in critical reviews and certain other noncommercial uses permitted by copyright law.

TABLE OF CONTENTS

INTRODUCTION 1

BENEFITS AND HISTORY 4

BREAKFAST RECIPES 6

CHAPTER ONE 7

    OVERNIGHT OATS WITH FRUIT 7

CHAPTER TWO 12

    PROTEIN-PACKED PANCAKES 12

LUNCH RECIPES 16

CHAPTER THREE 18

    EGG AND CHEESE BURRITO 18

CHAPTER FOUR 20

    AVOCADO AND TOMATO SANDWICH 20

CHAPTER FIVE 24

Mediterranean Couscous Salad 24

CHAPTER SIX 28
　　Turkey wrapped with Hummus 28

DINNER RECIPES 30

CHAPTER SEVEN 32
　　Grilled Salmon with Asparagus 32

CHAPTER EIGHT 36
　　Chicken and Broccoli Stir-Fry 36

CHAPTER NINE 40
　　Veggie Lasagna 40

SNACK RECIPES 43

CHAPTER TEN 44
　　Spicy Roasted Chickpeas 44

CHAPTER ELEVEN 48
　　Trail Mix 48

CHAPTER TWELVE 52
　　Greek Yogurt and Fruit Parfait 52

CONCLUSION 56

INTRODUCTION

Are you attempting to lose weight and get in better shape? You may find the Slim Fast diet to be a fantastic choice. A diet program called Slim Fast was created to assist people in losing weight swiftly and securely in a short period. The 1970s saw the introduction of this eating plan, which is still well-liked today.

The foundation of the Slim Fast diet is the recommendation to swap out two of your daily meals for a Slim Fast shake or bar. The diet's objective is to substitute lower-calorie, higher-protein, and higher-fiber meals for your regular ones. The shakes and bars are made to have a high protein content and a high fiber content while having fewer calories and fat.

A low-calorie diet is what the Slim Fast plan is all

about. You are advised to consume fewer calories than you would on a conventional diet. Eat fewer calories to force the body to burn fat for energy. This contributes to a decrease in body fat and total weight.

Regular exercise is also advised by the Slim Fast diet. This facilitates weight loss and enhances your general well-being and level of fitness.

The meals for the Slim Fast diet are created to be simple to prepare and to give you all the nourishment you need to be healthy. Most Slim Fast meals are high in protein, fiber, and other necessary elements but low in fat and calories. A wide range of nutritious components, including fruits, vegetables, lean meats, and healthy fats, are also used in meals.

A wonderful approach to get started on your weight loss journey is with the Slim Fast diet. It can help you achieve your weight loss objectives in a healthy and long-lasting way with its meals that are low in calories, high in protein, and rich in fiber. Therefore, the Slim Fast diet may be your best option if you're seeking a quick strategy to reduce weight and get in shape.

Keep in mind that the Slim Fast diet is neither a miraculous cure nor a quick fix. To achieve your goals, you must be committed and work hard. But with the correct diet and exercise routine, you can gradually get closer to your weight loss objectives. Therefore, don't be frightened to try the Slim Fast diet and discover how it works for you.

Wishing you luck as you work to lose weight!

BENEFITS AND HISTORY

Slim Fast has been helping people to lose weight for over 40 years. It has been a popular diet for those who are looking for a convenient solution to dieting.

Slim Fast is a meal replacement system that helps dieters reach their weight loss goals without having to count calories or follow a strict diet. It's a simple, one-step plan that simplifies dieting and helps dieters stay on track.

The Slim Fast diet plan includes meal replacement shakes, bars, and other snacks to help dieters make healthier food choices throughout the day. The shakes, bars, and snacks contain a balance of protein, carbohydrates, and healthy fats to help keep dieters feeling full and energized.

The Slim Fast diet plan is designed to help dieters lose weight quickly and safely. With a combination of low-calorie meal replacements, reduced portion sizes, and increased physical activity, dieters can achieve their weight loss goals in a short amount of time.

The benefits of the Slim Fast diet plan are numerous. It is convenient, easy to follow, and can help dieters lose weight quickly without sacrificing nutrition. It also encourages dieters to make healthier food choices, as the meal replacements are low in calories and contain a balance of nutrients.

The Slim Fast diet plan has helped thousands of people to successfully reach their weight loss goals. With a simple and easy-to-follow plan, it is easy to see why so many people have been successful with Slim Fast. With a variety of flavors to choose from, there's something for everyone on the Slim Fast diet plan.

Whether you are looking to lose weight quickly or just make healthier food choices, the Slim Fast diet plan is a great option. With a combination of meal replacements, reduced portion sizes, and increased physical activity, the Slim Fast diet plan is a safe and effective way to reach your weight loss goals.

BREAKFAST RECIPES

CHAPTER ONE

Overnight Oats with Fruit

When it comes to losing weight and living a healthy lifestyle, overnight oats with fruit on the Slim Fast diet can be a great way to start your day. By combining complex carbohydrates with a source of protein and healthy fats, overnight oats provide a balanced and nutritious breakfast that can help you stay fuller for longer and reach your weight loss goals.

Overnight oats with fruit on the Slim Fast diet are perfect for those who are short on time in the mornings. All you need to do is prepare the oats the night before and let them sit in the fridge overnight. Then, in the morning, you can top them with your favorite fruits and enjoy a wholesome breakfast that is packed with essential nutrients and vitamins.

One of the best things about overnight oats is that they are so versatile. You can mix and match different types of oats, fruits, and other ingredients to create delicious and nutritious recipes. Here is a basic recipe for overnight oats with fruit on the Slim Fast diet:

Ingredients:

- 1 cup rolled oats

- ½ cup skimmed milk

- 2 tablespoons honey

- 1 tablespoon chia seeds

- ½ cup fresh or frozen berries

- ¼ cup chopped nuts

- 1 teaspoon cinnamon

Instructions:

1. In a bowl, combine the oats, milk, honey, and chia seeds.

2. Cover the bowl and place it in the refrigerator overnight.

3. In the morning, top the oats with fresh or frozen berries and chopped nuts.

4. Sprinkle with cinnamon and enjoy.

This overnight oats with fruit recipe is a great way to start your day while following the Slim Fast diet. The oats provide complex carbohydrates to keep you full, while the chia seeds and nuts add healthy fats and protein. The honey and cinnamon provide some sweetness, while the berries add a burst of flavor and essential vitamins.

If you're looking for an even more delicious breakfast, you can also add other ingredients like nut butter, yogurt, or coconut flakes. You can also swap out the berries for other fruits like apples, pears, or bananas. The possibilities are endless.

Overnight oats with fruit on the Slim Fast diet are a great way to start your day and stay on track with your weight loss goals. They're easy to prepare and can be modified to fit any dietary restrictions. With a few basic ingredients, you can create a delicious and nutritious breakfast that will keep you full and satisfied all morning long.

CHAPTER TWO

Protein-Packed Pancakes

You've found the right place if you're seeking a delicious and protein-rich pancake recipe that's ideal for the Slim Fast diet. One of the most well-liked breakfast meals for a Slim Fast diet is protein-rich pancakes. They are not only scrumptious and filling, but they are also rich in vital nutrients that will keep you satiated and energized all day.

These protein-rich pancakes are created to be a healthy and nourishing breakfast alternative and are crafted with premium ingredients. Whole wheat flour, rolled oats, whey protein powder, baking powder, and a dash of salt make up the recipe's foundation. The pancakes' base is wholesome and nutritious thanks to this combination of components. These pancakes are a fantastic way to start the day with an energy boost because they are also loaded with protein from the whey protein powder.

Start by combining the dry ingredients in a medium bowl to make these protein-rich pancakes. Add the wet ingredients next, including the melted coconut oil, almond milk, and egg whites. Mix ingredients in a whisk until they are thoroughly blended. Then, apply non-stick cooking spray and heat a non-stick skillet over medium-high heat. Pour the batter into the skillet and cook for two to three minutes on each side, or until golden. Serve with your preferred garnishes, such as honey, nuts, or fresh fruit.

On a Slim Fast diet, these protein-rich pancakes are a fantastic way to start the day. They include vital vitamins, minerals, and proteins that will keep you satiated and energized all day. Additionally, they are simple to create and versatile enough to accommodate your preferred toppings. Try this tasty and wholesome meal for a protein-packed breakfast that is ideal for the Slim Fast program.

SLIM FAST DIET RECIPES

Ingredients:

- Half a cup of whole wheat flour

- 1/2 cup of rolled oats

- Whey protein powder, two scoops

- One teaspoon of baking soda

- Salt, a dash

One cup of almond milk

- 2 beaten egg whites

- 2 tablespoons of coconut oil, melted

Instructions:

1. Combine the dry ingredients in a medium bowl.

2. Add the wet ingredients and stir everything together thoroughly.

3. Spray nonstick cooking spray into a nonstick skillet

and heat it over medium-high heat.

4. Pour the batter into the skillet and cook for two to three minutes on each side, or until golden.

5. Top with your preferred garnishes, such as honey, almonds, or fresh fruit.

LUNCH RECIPES

DR. COLIN C. LONGENECKER

CHAPTER THREE

Egg and Cheese Burrito

Are you on a slim fast diet and looking for a delicious and nutritious breakfast option? Look no further than the Egg and Cheese Burrito on the Slim Fast Diet. This delicious burrito is packed with protein, fiber, and flavor. Not only is it a great way to start your day, but it's also a great way to stick to your diet plan.

Ingredients:

- 4 eggs
- ½ cup shredded cheese
- 2 tablespoons salsa
- 1 tablespoon butter
- 2 burrito-size whole wheat or low-carb tortillas
- Salt and pepper to taste

Instructions:

1. Heat a large skillet over medium-high heat and melt the butter.

2. Crack the eggs into the pan and scramble until they are cooked through.

3. Add the cheese, salsa, and salt and pepper to taste. Stir to combine.

4. Place the tortillas on a plate and spoon the egg and cheese mixture onto the center of each tortilla.

5. Fold one side of the tortilla over the filling and then fold the other side over to make a burrito.

6. Place the burritos on the skillet and cook for 2-3 minutes on each side until lightly golden brown.

7. Serve with your favorite toppings like lettuce, tomatoes, avocado, sour cream, or guacamole.

Enjoy your delicious Egg and Cheese Burrito on the Slim Fast Diet. This flavorful and nutritious breakfast option is sure to keep you full and energized throughout the day. Plus, it's easy to make and can be prepared in no time. So, if you're looking for a tasty and healthy breakfast option, this burrito is sure to hit the spot!

CHAPTER FOUR

Avocado and Tomato Sandwich

When it comes to healthy eating, the Slim Fast diet is one of the best. It is a popular diet plan that promises weight loss by restricting calorie and carbohydrate intake. The Slim Fast diet emphasizes eating real food, including lean proteins, vegetables, and fruits. One of the most popular Slim Fast diet recipes is the Avocado and Tomato Sandwich. This easy-to-make sandwich is packed full of nutrients and is sure to keep you satisfied.

Ingredients:

1 whole-wheat sandwich thin
2 tablespoons mashed avocado.
2 slices of tomato
1/4 cup shredded lettuce.
1 teaspoon olive oil
1/4 teaspoon garlic powder
1/4 teaspoon onion powder
Salt and pepper to taste.

Preparation:

1. Begin by toasting the sandwich thin in a toaster or an oven.

2. In a small bowl, mash the avocado with a fork until it is smooth. Spread the mashed avocado on one side of the toasted sandwich thin.

3. Place the tomato slices on top of the avocado and top with the shredded lettuce.

4. In a separate small bowl, mix the olive oil, garlic powder, onion powder, salt, and pepper. Drizzle the mixture over the sandwich.

5. Place the other side of the sandwich thin on top of the filling and press gently to secure.

6. Cut the sandwich into two halves and serve.

The Avocado and Tomato Sandwich is a great choice for a Slim Fast diet. It is full of healthy fats, protein, and fiber to keep you full and satisfied. The sandwich is easy to make and can be customized with any of your favorite vegetables or condiments. Enjoy this delicious sandwich as part of your Slim Fast diet plan and you will be sure to see results in no time.

So go ahead and make this delicious Avocado and Tomato Sandwich and start your Slim Fast diet plan today!

CHAPTER FIVE

Mediterranean Couscous Salad

If you are looking for a delicious and nutritious meal that also fits into your Slim Fast Diet, look no further than Mediterranean Couscous Salad. This flavorful dish is packed with healthy ingredients and will be sure to leave you feeling satisfied and energized.

This salad is a great way to get your daily dose of vegetables and protein. It is also a great source of fiber, which helps to keep you feeling full for longer. The combination of couscous, vegetables, and herbs make this a flavorful and unique meal that is sure to please.

To make this Mediterranean Couscous Salad, you will need the following ingredients: one cup of whole wheat couscous, one cup of cooked chickpeas, one cup of diced tomatoes, one cup of diced cucumber, one cup of diced red onion, one cup of diced bell pepper, two tablespoons of extra virgin olive oil, two tablespoons of lemon juice, one teaspoon of dried oregano, one teaspoon of dried basil, one teaspoon of garlic powder, one teaspoon of onion powder, one teaspoon of cumin, one teaspoon of paprika, one teaspoon of sea salt, and one teaspoon of black pepper.

To prepare the salad, start by bringing a pot of salted water to a boil. Add the couscous, reduce the heat to low, and simmer for about 10 minutes. Once the couscous is cooked, drain and transfer to a large bowl.

Next, add the chickpeas, tomatoes, cucumber, red onion, and bell pepper to the bowl. Drizzle the olive oil, lemon juice, and all the spices over the top and mix until everything is evenly distributed.

Finally, transfer the Mediterranean Couscous Salad to a large serving bowl and top it with some fresh herbs, such as parsley or cilantro. Serve it up with some fresh crusty bread and enjoy!

This Mediterranean Couscous Salad is a flavorful, nutrient-packed meal that fits into your Slim Fast Diet.

With its combination of healthy veggies, protein-packed chickpeas, and a zesty blend of herbs and spices, it is sure to be a hit with the whole family. So, what are you waiting for? Get cooking and enjoy!

DR. COLIN C. LONGENECKER

CHAPTER SIX

Turkey wrapped with Hummus.

Turkey wrap with hummus is a great way to add flavor and nutrition to your Slim Fast diet. This healthy, low-calorie wrap combines lean turkey slices with creamy hummus for a flavorful and satisfying meal. Not only does this meal provide essential nutrients, but it also helps you to stay on track with your Slim Fast diet.

Ingredients:
-1/2 cup prepared hummus
-2 large whole wheat tortillas
-4 ounces thinly sliced deli turkey

-1/4 cup diced red onion.

-1/4 cup diced cucumber.

-1/4 cup shredded lettuce.

-1/2 cup shredded carrots.

-Salt and pepper to taste

Instructions:

1. Spread the hummus over each of the tortillas.

2. Top with the turkey slices, red onion, cucumber, lettuce, and carrots.

3. Sprinkle with salt and pepper.

4. Roll up the tortillas and cut them in half.

5. Serve immediately or wrap in wax paper for later.

This turkey wrap with hummus is an easy and delicious meal that will help you stay on track with your Slim Fast diet. The combination of lean turkey and creamy hummus provides a filling and flavorful meal that is also low in calories and high in nutrition. The added vegetables add a variety of flavors and nutrients while the whole wheat tortilla gives your wrap a complex carbohydrate boost. Enjoy this wrap as part of your Slim Fast diet for a healthy and tasty meal.

SLIM FAST DIET RECIPES

DINNER RECIPES

DR. COLIN C. LONGENECKER

CHAPTER SEVEN

Grilled Salmon with Asparagus

Are you looking for a delicious and nutritious meal that fits your Slim Fast diet plan? Look no further than this delectable Grilled Salmon with Asparagus dish. This easy-to-make meal is the perfect way to get in all the nutrition you need while still enjoying a flavorful meal.

The ingredients for this delicious Slim Fast diet recipe include salmon fillets, asparagus, olive oil, garlic, lemon juice, salt, and pepper. To begin, preheat your grill to medium-high heat and lightly oil the grilling surface. Place the salmon fillets on the grill, and cook for about 4 minutes per side, or until the fish is cooked through.

Meanwhile, prepare the asparagus. Trim the tough ends of the asparagus and discard. Place the asparagus in a bowl, drizzle with olive oil, and sprinkle with garlic, lemon juice, salt, and pepper. Toss to combine, and then place the asparagus on the grill. Grill the asparagus for about 4 minutes, or until lightly charred and tender.

To serve, divide the grilled salmon and asparagus among four plates. Drizzle with a bit of olive oil and lemon juice. Serve with a side of your favorite Slim Fast diet-friendly side dish, such as a green salad or roasted vegetables.

This Grilled Salmon with Asparagus dish is a nutritious and delicious meal that's perfect for any Slim Fast diet plan. The flavors of the salmon and asparagus are enhanced by olive oil, garlic, lemon juice, salt, and pepper. Plus, the meal is easy to prepare and takes less than 30 minutes to make. Enjoy!

Nutrition Facts

Serving Size: 1 serving

Calories: 329

Fat: 16.3g

Carbohydrates: 6.8g

Protein: 37.2g

Fiber: 2.7g

Sugar: 2.1g

Sodium: 463mg

Cholesterol: 90mg

Enjoy your Grilled Salmon with Asparagus as part of your Slim Fast diet plan and get the nutrition you need to reach your weight loss goals. This delicious and nutritious meal is sure to please everyone at the table!

DR. COLIN C. LONGENECKER

CHAPTER EIGHT

Chicken and Broccoli Stir-Fry

A quick and easy supper that is both delicious and nourishing is chicken and broccoli stir-fry. For people following a slim fast diet who want to have a tasty, nutritious, and low-calorie supper, this recipe is ideal. Even the pickiest diners will be satiated by the unique blend of lean chicken, healthful broccoli, and tasty spices in this stir-fry.

The secret to producing this recipe is to use fresh, high-quality ingredients and lean chicken parts. Less fat and calories are present in leaner chicken. Cut into cubes or strips, boneless, skinless chicken breast would be a nice option. You can also use skinless, boneless chicken thighs if you'd like.

After being cleaned and trimmed of any brown spots or wilted leaves, the broccoli should be cut into small florets. It will be simpler to stir-fry florets that are smaller in size.

Once all of your ingredients are prepared, you may begin cooking. A sizable nonstick skillet should be heated to medium. Add the chicken, then a tablespoon of oil. Chicken should be cooked until no longer pink.

Add the broccoli and continue to stir-fry for an additional two to three minutes after the chicken is done. Add a teaspoon of garlic powder and a tablespoon of soy sauce. Stir-fry the broccoli for a further minute or two, or until it's soft but still crisp.

Stir-fry the cooked chicken for one or two more minutes after adding it. If necessary, taste the stir-fry and make spice adjustments. For a heartier dinner, serve with cooked brown rice or quinoa.

When you're on a slim quick diet, this chicken and broccoli stir-fry is a terrific dish to prepare. Despite being minimal in calories and fat, it is flavorful and nutritious. It is not only delicious but also quite simple to make. With little effort, a healthy lunch may be prepared and served in a matter of minutes. So the next time you're searching for a quick, wholesome supper for your diet, try this stir-fried chicken and broccoli recipe. You won't be let down!

Ingredients:

1-teaspoon oil
- 1 pound of cubed, skinless, boneless chicken breast
2-cups of broccoli florets
- A teaspoon of soy sauce
– One teaspoon of garlic powder

Instructions:

1. Put a big nonstick skillet on the stovetop at medium heat. Add the chicken after the oil. Cook the chicken until it stops being pink.

2. Stir-fry the broccoli for two to three minutes after adding it.

3. Stir-fry for a further minute or two after adding the soy sauce and garlic powder.

4. Include the cooked chicken and stir-fry for an additional one to two minutes. If necessary, taste and adjust the seasoning.

5. Serve with cooked quinoa or brown rice. Enjoy!

DR. COLIN C. LONGENECKER

CHAPTER NINE

Veggie Lasagna

A delicious, healthy, and light dish that is ideal for individuals following the Slim Fast diet is veggie lasagna. This recipe is minimal in calories and fat and is full of fiber and vegetables. It is the perfect lunch for busy dieters because it is also incredibly simple to prepare.

Use high-quality ingredients to create a tasty vegetable lasagna. Pick fresh products, especially veggies, for the greatest outcomes. You should choose low-fat, low-sodium cheese for the dish. Use either a homemade sauce or a low-sodium marinara sauce for the sauce.

Start by setting your oven to 375 degrees. Prepare the vegetables next. Wash and julienne any fresh veggies you intend to use. Thaw frozen vegetables before dicing if using them. Place the prepared vegetables in a separate container.

Make the lasagna noodles next. As directed on the packaging, cook the lasagna noodles. Drain the noodles once they are finished cooking, then reserve them.

It's time to put the lasagna together now. Start by spreading a thin layer of marinara sauce across the bottom of a baking dish. Lasagna noodles are placed on top, then a layer of julienned veggies. Before adding another layer of marinara sauce, sprinkle with low-fat cheese. The remaining sauce and cheese are placed on top, then a final layer of noodles.

After the lasagna is put together, cover it with foil and bake it for 25 minutes in the preheated oven. Remove the cover after 25 minutes and continue baking for a further 10 minutes, or until the cheese is melted and bubbling.

Before serving, take the lasagna out of the oven and allow it cool for ten minutes. Serve with steamed veggies or a side salad.

For people on the Slim Fast diet, vegetable lasagna is a fantastic dish. It is nutritious, flavorful, and light. It's also simple to prepare, which makes it the perfect supper for busy dieters. On the Slim Fast plan, eat veggie lasagna for a filling and tasty supper!

DR. COLIN C. LONGENECKER

SNACK RECIPES

CHAPTER TEN

Spicy Roasted Chickpeas

Spicy Roasted Chickpeas are a delicious and nutritious snack that is perfect for any Slim Fast diet. Chickpeas are a great source of protein, fiber, and vitamins, making them a great addition to any meal. Roasting them with spices adds a delightful flavor that will have you reaching for more.

Ingredients

- 2 cans of chickpeas, drained and rinsed
- 2 tablespoons olive oil
- 1 teaspoon paprika

- 1 teaspoon garlic powder
- 1 teaspoon cumin
- 1 teaspoon chili powder
- Salt and pepper, to taste

Preparation

1. Preheat oven to 400° F.

2. Place drained and rinsed chickpeas on a baking sheet and drizzle with olive oil.

3. Sprinkle with paprika, garlic powder, cumin, chili powder, salt, and pepper.

4. Toss to coat evenly.

5. Bake for 25 minutes, stirring halfway through.

6. Remove from oven and serve warm.

These Spicy Roasted Chickpeas are the perfect addition to any Slim Fast diet. They are full of protein and fiber, making them a great snack for weight loss. The spices add a delicious flavor that will have you reaching for more. Plus, they are easy to make and require minimal ingredients. Enjoy!

Nutrition

Serving Size: 1/2 cup
Calories: 140
Fat: 4.5g
Carbohydrates: 20g
Protein: 6g
Fiber: 6g

DR. COLIN C. LONGENECKER

CHAPTER ELEVEN

Trail Mix

Trail mix is a great snack option for those looking to add a little extra flavor and nutrition to their Slim Fast diet. This high-energy snack is packed with protein, fiber, and healthy fats, making it an ideal snack to help you stay full and satisfied between meals. With a variety of ingredients and endless possibilities, trail mix is a great way to get creative and get the nutrition you need without sacrificing flavor.

What is Trail Mix?

A trail mix is a combination of dried fruits, nuts, and

seeds that are usually enjoyed as a snack. The combination of ingredients provides a variety of flavors, textures, and nutrients, making it a great option for those looking for a nutritious and satisfying snack. The trail mix is high in protein, fiber, and healthy fats, making it a great choice for those trying to lose weight on a Slim Fast diet.

Ingredients for Trail Mix

There are no set recipes for trail mix and the ingredients can vary depending on your individual preferences. Generally, trail mix is made with a combination of nuts, dried fruits, and seeds. Some popular ingredients include almonds, cashews, peanuts, walnuts, pumpkin seeds, sunflower seeds, raisins, cranberries, and other dried fruits. Feel free to mix and match different ingredients to make a trail mix that is unique to you.

Preparation of Trail Mix

Making your trail mix is quick and easy. Start by combining your desired ingredients in a bowl and stirring until they are evenly distributed. Then, spread the mixture on a baking sheet lined with parchment paper and bake in the oven at 350°F for 10-15 minutes. This helps to make the ingredients crunchy and enhances their flavor. Once the trail mix is done baking, let it cool and then store it in an air-tight container or a resealable bag.

Health Benefits of Trail Mix

In addition to being a delicious snack, trail mix offers a variety of health benefits. The combination of nuts, seeds, and dried fruits provides essential vitamins and minerals as well as protein, fiber, and healthy fats. This combination of nutrients helps to keep you feeling full and satisfied between meals, making it a great option for those trying to lose weight on a Slim Fast diet.

Trail mix is a great snack option for those looking to add a little extra flavor and nutrition to their Slim Fast diet. This high-energy snack is packed with protein, fiber, and healthy fats, making it an ideal snack to help you stay full and satisfied between meals. With a variety of ingredients and endless possibilities, trail mix is a great way to get creative and get the nutrition you need without sacrificing flavor.

So, if you're looking for a delicious and nutritious snack to add to your Slim Fast diet, give trail mix a try. With its combination of protein, fiber, and healthy fats, it's sure to keep you full and satisfied between meals!

DR. COLIN C. LONGENECKER

CHAPTER TWELVE

Greek Yogurt and Fruit Parfait

If you're looking for a healthy, delicious breakfast that will keep you full and satisfied all morning, try this Greek Yogurt and Fruit Parfait on Slim Fast Diet Recipes. Rich in protein, low in calories, and packed with flavor, this parfait will help you stay on track with your weight loss goals while still enjoying a tasty treat.

Ingredients:

- 2 cups of Greek yogurt

- 1 cup of your favorite seasonal fruit (blueberries, strawberries, peaches, etc.), diced

- 1/4 cup of crushed almonds

- 1/4 cup of honey

- 1/4 teaspoon of cinnamon

- 1/4 cup of granola or muesli

- 2 tablespoons of chia seeds

Instructions:

1. In a medium bowl, combine the yogurt, diced fruit, crushed almonds, honey, and cinnamon.

2. Layer the yogurt mixture and granola in a parfait glass or bowl.

3. Sprinkle the chia seeds over the top of the parfait.

4. Serve chilled or at room temperature.

This simple and delicious Greek Yogurt and Fruit Parfait on Slim Fast Diet Recipes is sure to satisfy your taste buds. With a good balance of protein, healthy fats, and complex carbohydrates, it's a great way to start your day. Almonds and chia seeds provide healthy fats and fiber, while yogurt and fruit provide protein and carbohydrates. The honey and cinnamon add a touch of sweetness and flavor. This parfait is also a great snack option for any time of day.

Making this parfait is easy and can be done in just a few minutes. It's a great way to get more fruit and protein into your diet while still enjoying a delicious treat. If you're looking for a way to stay on track with your weight loss goals, this Greek Yogurt and Fruit Parfait on Slim Fast Diet Recipes is a great option. Enjoy!

DR. COLIN C. LONGENECKER

CONCLUSION

The Slim Fast diet recipes provide a variety of options for people looking to lose weight and stay healthy. They have a wide range of ingredients and preparations that allow for great versatility, so anyone can find something that works for them. The recipes are designed to be quick and easy to make, so even busy individuals can whip up delicious meals in no time. The shakes and bars provide a convenient way to get in all the necessary nutrients.

The Slim Fast diet recipes offer an easy way to drop pounds and get in shape. All the recipes are full of nutritious ingredients that are designed to help people reach their weight loss goals. The recipes are also designed to be low in saturated fat, sodium, and added sugars. This makes them a great choice for those looking to maintain a healthier lifestyle.

In addition to the recipes, the Slim Fast diet also includes shakes, bars, and other snacks. These are great for those looking to get in their daily dose of nutrients while on the go. The shakes and bars provide a convenient way to get in all the necessary vitamins and minerals.

Overall, the Slim Fast diet is a great option for those looking to lose weight and get in shape. The recipes are easy to make and provide a variety of options for all types of diets. Additionally, they are full of nutritious ingredients that are designed to help people reach their weight loss goals. The shakes and bars provide a convenient way to get in all the necessary nutrients. With the variety of options available, the Slim Fast diet is a great choice for anyone looking to slim down and get healthy.

This concludes the Slim Fast diet recipes book. We hope that you found it helpful and that you can use it to reach your weight loss goals.

SLIM FAST DIET RECIPES

www.ingramcontent.com/pod-product-compliance
Lightning Source LLC
Chambersburg PA
CBHW070320220526
45465CB00013B/1913